A GUIDE
NAVAJO WEAVINGS

by Kent McManis & Robert Jeffries

To Bill & Kathleen
Best of Rugs!
Kent McManis
Bob Jeffries
Jan. 8, 1999

Photography by Robin Stancliff

TREASURE CHEST BOOKS
TUCSON, ARIZONA

ACKNOWLEDGMENTS

We wish to thank many people for their help with this project. First, we would like to thank Laurie McManis for her patience, many suggestions, and hard work without which we could not have completed the book. Special gratitude goes to Jed Foutz for his enthusiastic encouragement, extra efforts, and friendship and to Bruce McGee for his continued support and uncommon kindness. Our appreciation also goes to Bruce Burnham, Robert Ingeholm, Georgianna Kennedy Simpson, Terry De Wald, Jackson Clark II, and Bill Malone for their invaluable information. As always, kudos to Robin Stancliff for her special talents. Our heartfelt thanks to all the weavers who have so generously shared their knowledge of weaving techniques and their personal histories with us over the years. And last but not least, we owe a special debt of gratitude to Barbara Teller Ornelas for her input, time, wisdom, and selfless spirit.

TREASURE CHEST BOOKS
P. O. Box 5250
Tucson, AZ 85703-0250
(520) 623-9558

ISBN 1-887896-07-4
Library of Congress catalog card number 97-60805

Title page photo: detail from rug by Daisy Nakai, Figure 19.

Rugs courtesy of Shiprock Trading Company: Figures 9, 12, 14, 15, 19, 20, 30, 32, 43, 44, 47, and back cover.
Rugs courtesy of Twin Rocks Trading Post: Figures 17, 28, 49, and 50.
Rugs courtesy of Blair's Dinnebito Trading Post: Figures 29, 51, and 52.
Rugs courtesy of Terry De Wald: Figures 1, 2, 4, and 6.
Rugs courtesy of private collections: Figures 3 and 10.
All other rugs are courtesy of Grey Dog Trading Company.

This book is set in Bitstream Charter and ITC Goudy Sans.
Edited by Linnea Gentry
Designed by Paul Mirocha
Printed in Korea

CONTENTS

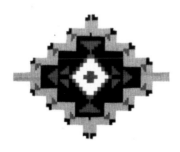

SPIDER WOMAN'S GIFT

WEAVING IS AT THE HEART OF BEING for many Navajo women, an essential part of their lives that is both vital to them individually and vital to their lives within their community. While hunting and raiding were originally within the man's realm in early times, weaving became primarily the woman's domain. The use of the portable loom allowed a woman to tend her sheep, watch her children, and weave simultaneously. Over the years, weaving came to play a crucial role in female relationships and in instilling shared values and structure in the Navajo community. As such, this skill has become a source of personal pride for the Navajo woman and enhanced the respect from her people. Its practitioners today still perpetuate their tribal traditions while reflecting a dramatically transformed way of life.

The Navajo believe that the gift of weaving was taught to them by Spider Woman, one of the Navajo Holy People. Spider Woman originally showed Changing Woman (another holy person) how to weave, with the stipulation that she would in turn teach the Navajo. Spider Man showed them how to make the loom and tools out of sacred Navajo stones and shells (turquoise, jet, white shell, and abalone), as well as with the earth, sun, rain, and sky themselves. This important connection to the earth and elements is characteristic of the Navajo respect and reverence for the natural world. It also demonstrates the significance of weaving within the Navajo religion.

Along with the belief in the sacred origin of weaving, many Navajo give credence to specific taboos. While a number of younger weavers no longer follow them and some beliefs seem purely localized, many weavers still heed these traditions. The weavers of some regions still incorporate the famous spirit trail, or weaver's pathway, near the finish of their rugs. (See chapter four.) Many artists feel that designing rugs with Navajo deities, called Yé'ii (YEH-ee), snakes, or bears is sacrilegious. Setting down tools while weaving or leaving them in the loom when not weaving is believed by some to bring misfortune.

Some weavers don't weave at night; some don't weave while pregnant. Some think it unacceptable to joke about weaving, since it is a serious endeavor. Some weavers sing songs about their rugs while weaving to ensure success. Many also pray before, during, and after creating a piece to aid their current work and future endeavors.

While weaving itself may not be intended to perform a specific religious act, it is rooted in the traditions of the Navajo people and therefore imbued with the sacred. Navajo religion revolves around beauty and harmony within their universe; a splendid Navajo rug represents these aspects of their world view in an appropriately beautiful and lasting form.

The majority of weavers we know today started at an early age, many before they were ten years old. As is typical in a matrilineal society, most learned from their mothers and grandmothers. Some have woven for most of their lives; some go for long periods without weaving. A pattern we have found among several weavers is exemplified by noted artist Barbara Teller Ornelas. As with all traditional Navajo women, Barbara was expected to weave and, although she resisted, was taught to weave by the age of eight by her mother. She experimented occasionally but did not come to fully appreciate and enjoy her ability, however, until years later when her husband, David Ornelas, saw the special quality in her talent and encouraged her to weave full time. Barbara, in turn, is now teaching her daughter, Sierra, her skills.

In the following chapters, we follow the development of Navajo weaving from past to present, tracing how the art has changed over the centuries and where it appears to be headed in the years to come. We also examine how a Navajo rug is made and what to look for when purchasing one. Above all, we hope to convey the respect and appreciation we feel towards Navajo weavers and admiration for their endurance in continuing an art of great beauty.

Detail of Transitional Period weaving in Figure 5.

The Navajo call themselves Diné
(dih-NEH), meaning "The People." The word "Navajo" is probably the Spanish
version of a Tewa* word: navahu ("nava" meaning field and "hu" meaning
large arroyo). This name stems from the fact that some early Navajo farmed
large watershed areas in their original northern New Mexico territory.
(See map, page 8.)

When did the Navajo arrive in the American Southwest? No two historians
or anthropologists seem to agree. It is generally accepted that these
Athapaskan-speaking people came sometime between 1000 and 1500 AD
from western Canada. Their linguistic cousins, the Apache, may have arrived
slightly earlier. They were certainly there before the Spanish arrived in the mid
1500s.

The Pueblo Indian peoples had been weaving for several centuries by the
time the Navajo appeared in the Arizona-New Mexico region. They wove gar-
ments and blankets made of cotton which had been introduced from Mexico
by 800 AD. The Navajo adopted cotton for their own weaving as their Pueblo
neighbors taught them the skill. Which Pueblo tribe or tribes were the teach-
ers is unclear. In most pueblos, men were the weavers. However, among the
Navajo the art of weaving was originally practiced by women. The cause of
this change may have been indirectly brought about by the attempts of the
Pueblo peoples to escape the Spanish domination. Primarily during the seven-
teenth century, many Pueblo people moved away from the Rio Grande Valley
region into the territory of the Navajo to the north and west. As the Pueblo
and Navajo peoples lived together and undoubtedly intermarried, it is easy to
see how a Pueblo man could have taught his Navajo wife to weave. The
Pueblos temporarily succeeded in the Great Revolt of 1680 against the
Spanish, after a century of Spanish demands for tributes and repression of
their native religions. After the Spanish reconquest of New Mexico in 1692,
even more Pueblo people escaped to the Navajo lands.

*Tewa (TAY-wah): a Pueblo Indian people and language

While the Navajo probably learned weaving in the mid 1600s, Spanish reports verify that they were weaving by 1700. This is considered the beginning of the Classic Period of Navajo weaving.

Although Spanish rule was harsh, it introduced certain benefits to the Navajo, most notably the horse and the sheep. The Navajo soon started raiding Spanish settlements to get them. Like other nomadic peoples, the Navajo benefited from the greater mobility of the horse. The sheep gave them both a new food source and a new material for weaving. By 1800, wool had virtually replaced cotton in Navajo textile production.

As the practice of weaving spread, indigo blue dye (derived from the indigo plant) became a popular trade item from the Spanish to the Navajo. Another important item brought by the Spanish was bayeta (by-YET-ah), a wool trade cloth originally from England, where it was called baize. It traveled

The Navajo lands consist of an area larger than the state of West Virginia and extend over the Four Corners area of Arizona, New Mexico, and Utah. (The reservation does not cross over into Colorado.) The Navajo tribe is the second largest in the country, numbering over 225,000 people.

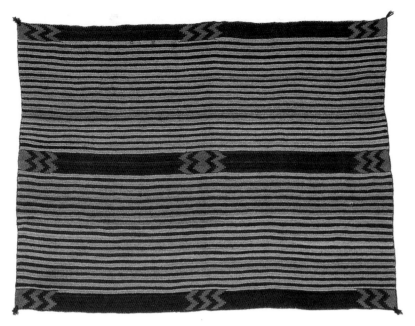

Figure 1. Second-phase chief's blanket variation, circa 1865. 52½ x 40 in.
This blanket has zig-zag red areas instead of bars. It was woven using natural grey
and brown, cochineal-dyed raveled red, and indigo-dyed blue yarns.

through Spain to Mexico and then north to New Mexico, first appearing there
in the late 1700s. The bayeta was commercially woven and dyed red with
either lac (from Old World tree-scale insects) or cochineal (from New World
cactus insects). The Navajo did not use the bayeta as it was but raveled it and
respun the wool to use in their own weavings.

Mexican independence from Spain in 1821 reversed the protectionist poli-
cies of the Spanish government. This allowed new trade channels between the
outside world and the Navajo of the New Mexican Territory. Independence
also provided an expanded market for Navajo weavings, including the famed
chief's blankets. The name of these blankets was a misnomer, as the Navajo
did not have chiefs. But many of these weavings did make their way to pow-
erful and well-to-do Plains Indians. First-phase chief's blankets appeared
around 1800 and consisted of a simple, grouped stripe design in indigo, white,
and dark brown. Before 1850, the second-phase chief's blanket design had
added a dozen pairs of red bars to the striped areas. (FIG. 1) Finally, by 1860

Figure 2. Third-phase chief's blanket variation, circa 1865. 71½ x 54 in. The typical wide background striping is overshadowed by the diamonds in this piece. It was made of natural white and brown, lac- and cochineal-dyed raveled red, and indigo-dyed blue yarns.

the third-phase chief's blanket generally substituted nine whole or partial diamonds to replace the bars. (FIG. 2)

Navajo weavers created many other varieties of wearing blankets during the Classic Period. These included the so-called Moki (MO-kee) blankets, Moki being the Spanish name for Hopi. This style consisted of a dark-brown and indigo-blue striped background on which were superimposed more and more elaborate red designs. While the Navajo undoubtedly copied this striped design from their Pueblo neighbors, the Hopi were not especially known for this particular color scheme in their striped blankets. (FIG. 3)

When New Mexico became United States territory after the Mexican War in 1848, the on-again-off-again raiding between the Navajo and the New Mexicans became an American problem. Unfortunately, the New Mexicans were usually not held accountable for their part in these conflicts as the Navajo were. Several treaties signed between some bands of Navajo and the U.S. Government ended in failure because leaders of these bands had no authority to speak for other Navajos. There was no one leader with whom the Americans could have negotiated to bring all the Navajo together.

In 1863, American forces under Kit Carson began a scorched-earth campaign, destroying the Navajo crops and slaughtering their sheep. The Navajo were rounded up and forced into confinement at Bosque Redondo near Fort Sumner, New Mexico. Many died on the infamous Long Walk to Fort Sumner, and many more perished of disease while at the internment camp. The government's attempts to induce the Navajo to farm at Fort Sumner failed. Maintenance costs and other problems at the camp became excessive, exacerbated by graft and theft by outsiders. In 1868, the government allowed the Navajo to return to their homeland with a new treaty. Of the over 8,000 Navajo held at Bosque Redondo, over 2,000 had died. The Bosque Redondo

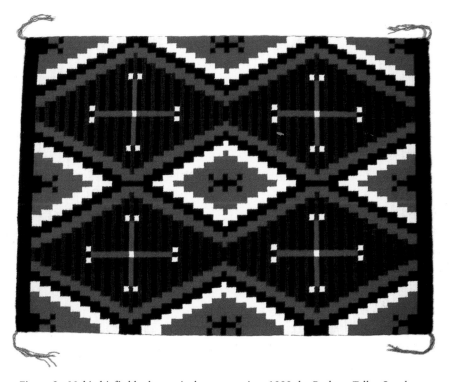

Figure 3. Moki chief's blanket revival tapestry, circa 1990, by Barbara Teller Ornelas. 26 x 18 in. This weaving is a true tapestry with 92 wefts per inch.

debacle is to the Navajo people one of the most tragic and formative episodes in their history.

Several events occurred at Bosque Redondo that would also change the face of Navajo weaving. Along with the Army rations, the Navajos were given blankets produced by the Spanish weavers of New Mexico, blankets with serrated diamond designs derived from the famous Saltillo (sawl-TEE-yo) textiles of northern Mexico. Up until this point, Navajo patterns consisted primarily of stripes and terraced figures. With this introduction, serrated patterns were quickly adopted by Navajo weavers.

The fact that the Navajo had lost almost all of their remaining sheep at Bosque Redondo was another pivotal event. The government replaced about 15,000 sheep and goats as part of the treaty, but with a new breed. Originally, the Navajo had raided churro sheep from the Spanish, a breed with long, silky wool that produces a fine yarn for weaving. The Americans replaced them with merino sheep which have a short, kinky wool that is greasy and difficult to clean as well as hard to spin and weave. This led to a deterioration in the quality of wool available for handspinning. As a result, the Navajo became more and more dependent on commercially spun yarn. From Europe came three-ply Saxony yarn, available before Bosque Redondo along with the bayeta. At the camp, Navajo weavers were introduced to commercially spun and dyed, three-ply Germantown yarn. Famous for its many bright colors, it was so named because most of the woolen mills producing it were in or near Germantown, Pennsylvania. This was largely replaced by four-ply Germantown yarn in the 1870s. (FIG. 4) The deep red cochineal-dyed bayeta cloth was supplanted about this time by aniline-dyed (coal tar dyes), orange-red American flannel. This new cloth was raveled as the bayeta had been. The use of indigo dye also started to diminish and virtually ceased by the 1890s.

All of these changes during or just after Bosque Redondo signaled the end of the Classic Period of weaving and ushered in the Transitional Period. Navajo textiles were changing in several ways. Much of this transformation was brought about by Anglo traders who immediately started setting up operations on or around the new Navajo reservation after 1868. They traded coffee and other staples plus, by the late 1870s, individual dye packets that increased the color palette weavers could use in their handspun textiles. In

Figure 4. Germantown weaving, circa 1880. 53 x 36 in. This textile has both three- and four-ply commercial aniline-dyed yarns. It is also fringed, common in Germantown weavings but extremely rare in other Navajo rugs.

return, the Navajo traded back weavings and wool. The traders soon began to influence the types of weavings produced. Americans wanted floor rugs and decorative weavings rather than blankets to wear. In the 1880s, the arrival of the railroad (and with it, tourists) increased this demand for rugs. Navajo weavers began to use designs with borders to provide the framing effect tourists liked. Serrated pattern, "eye-dazzler" weavings with many vibrant, outlined colors in zig-zag designs became popular. Thus, by the 1890s, Navajo weavings had changed from blankets to rugs and from personal items to saleable trade goods. (FIG. 5)

Other factors had also begun to affect Navajo weaving. The sheep that the government had given to the Navajo had grown to nearly two million. The Pendleton Woolen Mills opened in Oregon in the 1890s, and their relatively inexpensive, commercially made blankets virtually eliminated the need for Navajo-woven blankets. These events led reservation traders to encourage the use of handspun wool in weaving (because it was readily available and less expensive than imported, commercially spun yarns) and to concentrate even more on marketing rugs. The most important change was brought about by traders taking a more direct role in improving the quality of Navajo weaving.

One of the first traders to strongly encourage the Navajo to produce higher-quality weavings was Juan Lorenzo Hubbell. Hubbell took over the Ganado (gah-NAH-doe) Trading Post in Arizona in the late 1870s and refused to buy any rug with a commercial cotton string *warp* (the "skeleton" on which a rug is woven). Weavers had sometimes used cotton instead of handspun wool to save time, but the cotton warps often broke, weakening the structure of the rug. Hubbell also discouraged the use of multiple bright colors, persuading Ganado weavers to produce rugs with natural wool colors and a deep aniline red. He helped weavers return to designs of the Classic Period by having Anglo artists paint examples of the earlier blankets and then hanging them in his post for the weavers to use as guides. Thus Hubbell created some of the first revival weavings, including chief's-blanket and wearing-blanket styles done as rugs. The weavers also began incorporating old elements like equilateral crosses (later called Hubbell crosses by many people). By 1902, Hubbell was marketing Ganado area weavings through the Fred Harvey Company, the famous concessionaire of the Santa Fe Railroad. Since the company shared his appreciation for quality, the demand for improvement in Navajo weaving increased.

John B. Moore of the Crystal Trading Post in New Mexico also instigated new styles of weaving in the mid 1890s. His designs may have been drawn from some traditional sources, but many had obvious influences from Oriental rug designs. (FIG. 6) And some were undoubtedly all his own. In addition to introducing new design ideas, Moore also strove to improve the quality of wool used by the Crystal region's artists. At the time, many traders bought and sold rugs by the pound. This, of course, encouraged some weavers not to clean the grease from their wool, thus adding weight. Some even packed sand and dirt into their rugs! The practice gave rise to the notorious "pound blankets." To produce a higher grade of rug, Moore sent wool out to be professionally cleaned before giving it to his better weavers. (However, he did sell some

Figure 5. Transitional Period weaving, circa 1890. 78 x 49 in. Handspun aniline-dyed yarns are used in this piece. Note the use of both Classic Period terraced and later serrated diamond elements with a design strongly reminiscent of chief's blanket patterns.

poorer grade rugs by the pound.) Interestingly, Moore was one of the first to produce a mail-order catalog of rug styles for sale in both 1903 and 1911.

By the turn of the twentieth century, the Transitional Period had virtually ended. Blankets disappeared and use of Germantown yarns was also discontinued soon after. Navajo weaving was about to develop a more regional flavor as traders strove to find new markets for rugs.

Figure 6. Crystal weaving, circa 1910. 76½ x 50 in.
The Oriental rug influence is obvious.

NAVAJO WEAVING
IN THE TWENTIETH CENTURY

Trading posts began to proliferate
on the Navajo Reservation around the turn of the century. And although
traders came and went, many had a lasting impact on Navajo weaving. In this
chapter, we will examine both the regional styles and the styles developed by
individual weavers in the twentieth century and how some of both types came
to be. (Unless designated otherwise, all rugs illustrated in this and subsequent
chapters were woven in the 1990s.)

Ganado, Two Grey Hills,
and Burntwater Weavings

Several regional styles have similar patterns, although their color schemes are
different. An obvious starting point must be Ganado and the legacy of Juan
Lorenzo Hubbell. The deep red background of Ganado's early weavings has
continued to the present day, and a "Ganado Red" is still what many people
think of as a Navajo rug. In general, the Ganado area design consists of one
or two terraced diamonds in the center, with terraced triangles in each corner.
The patterns are also bordered. Colors consist of red, grey, white, black, and
sometimes shades of brown. Traditionally, the red and black were aniline-
dyed, and the other colors were from the natural wool. Today most are woven
with commercially dyed yarn. (FIG. 7)

The weavers in the nearby area of Klagetoh produce a style similar to
Ganado's but with a predominantly red pattern on a grey background.
However, many Ganado rugs have this same color scheme. As contemporary
weavers do fancier multiple borders, the question becomes what is the main
pattern and what is the true background? (FIG. 8)

Figure 7. Ganado weaving by Beth Tapaha. 72½x 49½ in.
This exemplifies the deep red background long associated with this area.

Similar in design but much more subdued in color are the famous Two Grey Hills weavings. Although Two Grey Hills patterns probably had roots in John B. Moore's Crystal rugs, two traders helped develop this specific style. One was Ed Davies, who purchased the Two Grey Hills Trading Post in 1909, and the other was George Bloomfield, who became the resident trader at nearby Toadlena (tode-LEE-nah) at about the same time. Both worked diligently with their area's weavers to develop better weavings. By the mid 1920s, the Two Grey Hills style was well established. The weavers preferred the browns, greys, and whites of natural sheep wool along with a dyed aniline black, rather than the red of Ganado weavers. The over-all patterns originally had stacked design elements but over the years became one or two terraced diamonds with terraced corner triangles in a bordered rug. Today, backgrounds are either grey, white, or shades of brown. (FIG. 9)

Burntwater weavings are an additional type using bordered patterns with central, terraced diamonds. Unlike the others, they comprise a relatively new style. Weaver Philomena Yazzie is credited with creating the first such rug in 1968, using vegetal-dyed colors (plant sources for the dyes). Burntwater trader Don Jacobs encouraged this innovation, and the *Arizona Highways* rug

Figure 8. Ganado weaving by Katherine Nez. 70 x 47 in. This is the type of textile referred to as a Klagetoh weaving by many dealers.

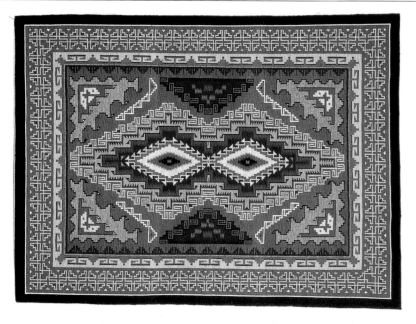

Figure 9. Two Grey Hills weaving by Rita Bedah. 72½ x 53 in.
The intricacy of the pattern shows a level of difficulty unusual even for this area.

issue of July 1974 made it famous. Early Burntwater weavings had fewer colors (perhaps 8 to 10) and less intricate patterns than they do today. By the mid 1980s, Bruce Burnham of Sanders, Arizona, was encouraging weavers in the area to include as many as forty colors per rug. Some Burntwater-style weavers still use vegetal-dyed wool, but many have gone over to commercially dyed yarns. (FIG. 10)

OTHER BORDERED STYLES

Two styles of Navajo weaving have evolved in the Four Corners area: Teec Nos Pos (TEES-nahs-PAHS) and Red Mesa. Around 1900, designs influenced by those of Oriental rugs became synonymous with Teec Nos Pos weavings. Hambleton Bridger Noel, the region's trader at the time, took no credit for the development. Some claim a missionary developed the ideas, and some believe the motifs were derived from some of John B. Moore's Crystal rugs. Elaborately figured borders, double-cross patterns, Xs, and hooked figures in a wide range of bright colors are their trademarks. Weavers also now produce somewhat less busy designs and more subtle colors to keep up with a changing rug market. Before World War II, most Teec Nos Pos rugs were woven with handspun yarn. Afterwards, commercial yarn became prominent. (FIG. 11)

Red Mesa outline rugs, as they are often called, are clearly derived from the eye-dazzler textiles of the Transitional Period. They have multiple, stacked, serrated diamonds outlined in different colors, sometimes with borders containing figured elements. Some people do not consider Red Mesa as a separate type from Teec Nos Pos, even though their origins are clearly different. (FIG. 12)

The storm pattern rug is another bordered design that may have developed in the fertile mind of Moore. Such a rug appeared in his 1911 catalog, in which he claimed its connection to Navajo mythology. Alternatively, the pattern's source may lie in a logo on the tags of flour-sacks sold on the

Figure 10. Burntwater tapestry by Barbara Teller Ornelas, circa 1990. 30 x 18½ in. This amazing tapestry has, on average, 92 wefts per inch as well as an elaborate design.

Figure 11. Teec Nos Pos weaving by Pearl Ben. 81½ x 59 in. Note the multiple colors, figured double borders, and complex pattern associated with Teec Nos Pos textiles.

Figure 12. Red Mesa outline weaving by Jason Harvey. 53 x 36 in. The "eye-dazzler" effect is muted by the softer colors.

Figure 13. Storm pattern weaving by Elsie Whitehorse. 24 x 19 in.
This shows the classic storm pattern in its most basic form.

reservation. Some have attributed it to a trader around 1900 at Red Lake Trading Post in the Western Reservation. For many years, the Western Reservation area produced most of the storm pattern rugs. Many stories about the "symbolic" and "religious" meanings of the storm pattern have been told. Whether any of them reflect true Navajo beliefs is questionable. (FIG. 13)

THE BANDED STYLES

Horizontally banded patterns developed in three regions. The first was in Chinle (CHIN-leh) at the mouth of Canyon de Chelly (duh SHAY). In the early 1920s, trader L. H. "Cozy" McSparron, with the help of patron Mary Cabot Wheelwright, sought a return to the old Classic Period of banded styles without borders. This began another revival cycle in Navajo weaving. McSparron and Wheelwright also prompted experimentation with plant dyes. While Navajo weavers had used vegetal dyes as far back as the early nineteenth century, there were never more than a few (yellow, green, and reddish brown) in common usage by the twentieth century. In 1940, Nonabah Bryan, a Navajo weaving teacher, wrote a pamphlet on how to create eighty-four plant dyes. Chinle weavings continue in the banded style in earth-tone colors, but their identification by pattern has become difficult at best, as they share many characteristics with Wide Ruins and Crystal textiles.

After purchasing the Wide Ruins Trading Post in 1938 and seeing the success of Chinle rugs, William and Sallie Lippincott also encouraged area weavers in the banded style. Of utmost importance to the Lippincotts was quality. Wide Ruins rugs incorporated more colors and intricate designs than those from Chinle. (FIG. 14) They featured a bead stitch of alternating *weft* colors, sometimes referred to as "railroad tracks," in some of the bands. (The weft is the succession of visible threads going across the face of the weaving.) Nearby Pine Springs weavers produce a very similar style but usually include a fair amount of green in the pattern. Many people do not recognize Pine Springs as a regional style.

Figure 14. Wide Ruins weaving by Peggy Lynch. 52½ x 36½ in. Atypically, the serrated banded patterns do not extend to the edges of this rug.

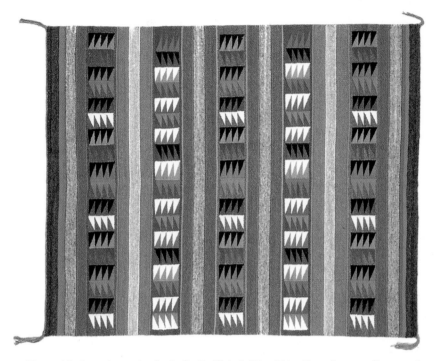

Figure 15. Crystal weaving by Lydia Peshlakai. 57 x 47 in. Note the wavy line panels versus the "bead stitch" elements of the Wide Ruins textile.

J. B. Moore's Crystal Trading Post went through several traders after he left in 1911. The old style of Crystal rug with its elaborately figured designs disappeared over time. In 1944, Don Jensen took over the post and promoted banded pattern weaving. The area's weavers developed a wavy line effect in most of their banded designs and still use it today. (FIG. 15)

PICTORIAL WEAVINGS

A wide variety exists in pictorial weavings. Many developed through experimentation, while others are rooted in Navajo religion. The real impetus behind their evolution has long been the trader.

Weavings with pictorial elements may have first appeared as early as the 1840s. Four small birds can be seen on a wearing blanket owned by the

Cheyenne chief White Antelope when he was killed at the Sand Creek Massacre in 1864. A photograph dated to 1873 shows a Navajo weaver with a United States flag-design rug she had made. By the 1880s and 90s, textiles with trains, animals, people, and letters from the alphabet started to appear. At first these were usually only floating design elements. (FIG. 16) But soon the pictorial pattern became the main focus of the weaving, and some featured fully developed scenes.

Figure 16. Pictorial weaving, circa 1940. 46 x 46 in. The "floating" bull and cow heads exemplify early pictorial design placement.

Yé'ii (YEH-ee) figures appeared on rugs before the turn of the century. (A Yé'ii is a Navajo holy person or deity.) At first, the Navajo considered putting a Yé'ii into a rug design taboo. Near the turn of the century Navajo weaver Yanapah, married to Richard Simpson (a trader near Farmington, New Mexico), wove large, single- and double-figure, vertical Yé'ii rugs. (The figures were standing upright as the rug was being woven.) Today, traders Steve and Georgianna Kennedy Simpson of Bluff, Utah, (no relation to Richard Simpson) are trying to revive this style of Yé'ii rug. The first "Simpson Yé'ii" revival was woven in 1995 by Anita Hatathle. (FIG. 17)

Yé'ii rugs developed in two other regions a few years after the turn of the century. At Shiprock, New Mexico, trader Will Evans helped develop multiple-figure Yé'ii weavings in the 1920s. They usually had white or light-colored backgrounds with several figures positioned horizontally across the rug as it was being woven. (The figures stood upright when the rug was turned sideways after weaving.) They had a multitude of bright, aniline-dyed colors and frequently used a great deal of commercial yarn. In the Lukachukai (LOO-kah-CHEW-kye) area, a similar horizontal Yé'ii rug developed, but was generally larger and somewhat coarser from the use of handspun yarn. They usually had darker backgrounds and more subdued colors. Today there is virtually no distinction as to which region a Yé'ii rug comes from. Many kinds of new border treatments and colors are prevalent. Yé'ii weavings often have a rainbow Yé'ii or guardian surrounding three sides of the other Yé'ii. (FIG. 18)

An interesting variation of the Yé'ii rug is the Yé'ii Bicheii (YEH-ee bih-SHAY). It was most likely developed in the Shiprock area near the turn of the century to depict the Nightway ceremony in which Navajo dancers portray Yé'ii Bicheii and other Yé'ii. Yé'ii Bicheii is called Talking God or Grandfather of the Gods. He appears in a white face mask as the lead dancer with other Yé'ii at the winter Night Chant (or Nightway) on the final night of the nine-day curative ceremony. Frequently any Yé'ii is incorrectly called a Yé'ii Bicheii, but most of the other Yé'ii are distinguised by blue masks. (FIG. 19)

Yé'ii figures also often appear in the famous sandpainting rugs. Sandpaintings themselves are created on the ground by Navajo *hataalii* (ha-TATH-lee), or medicine men, as part of their healing rituals. There is a multitude of these ceremonial chantways, or "sings" as they are often called, each

Figure 17. Simpson Yé'ii revival weaving by Marjorie Dee. 60 x 34 in. Note the vertical layout of the textile as opposed to the horizontal layout of the rug in Figure 18.

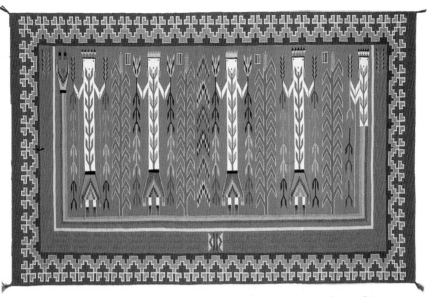

Figure 18. Yé'ii weaving by Rose Yazzie. 71½ x 47½ in. The Rainbow Yé'ii is shown in a U shape around the other Yé'ii.

Figure 19. Yé'ii Bicheii weaving by Daisy Nakai. 38 x 27½ in. The white-faced figure at the head of the line is the Yé'ii Bicheii, while the others are Yé'ii.

with its own set of sandpaintings. Because of their sacred nature, it was considered taboo for anyone other than a shaman to recreate them, at the risk of blindness or severe illness. In 1919, Franc Newcomb (the wife of trader Arthur Newcomb of Newcomb, New Mexico) convinced a hataalii named Hosteen Klah (HAHS-teen claw) to weave a sandpainting rug for her. Since he was a medicine man, Hosteen Klah did not have the same prohibition against reproducing it that other weavers had. Klah also convinced his nieces, Gladys and Irene Manuelito, to weave them. Several of their rugs were woven

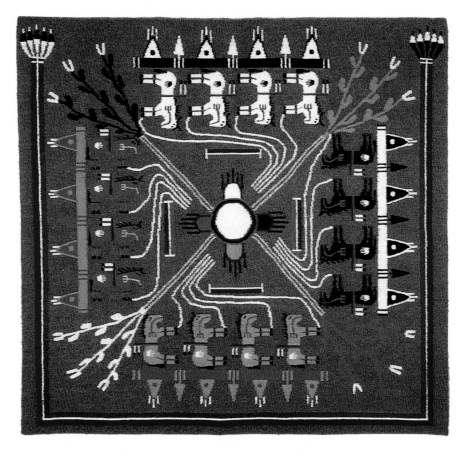

Figure 20. Sandpainting weaving by Mary Rose Tyler. 52½ x 49 in. This weaving is a version of the Home of the Buffalo sandpainting.

Figure 21. Pictorial weaving by Marie Begay. 27 x 25½ in. The four seasons (clockwise from upper left: winter, spring, summer, and fall) are shown in this older-style reservation scene.

Figure 22. Pictorial weaving by Virginia Nez. 33 x 32½ in. This is the newer style of pictorial weaving, also depicting a scene from reservation life.

Figure 23. Bird pictorial weaving by Alice Nockideneh.
35 x 23 in. This version has the birds on a corn stalk with
the wedding basket at the base.

for Mary Cabot Wheelwright and are now housed in the Wheelwright Museum in Santa Fe. A few weavers today still weave sandpainting rugs, often hiring a medicine man to perform a ceremony before or after the rug is woven to ensure protection. Payment for this ceremony adds to the price of an already intricately patterned and, hence, time-consuming and costly weaving. (FIG. 20)

Scenic pictorial rugs started to appear in the 1930s. Reservation life is the most common subject today, showing ceremonies or daily activities, depicted in two styles. The older and simpler style is woven in several areas of the reservation and treats the figures in a more naive, two-dimensional style of representation. Objects are often not shown in perspective regarding size to distance. (FIG. 21) The newer style was started in the 1970s by Linda Nez of Cedar Ridge, Arizona. Several members of the Nez extended family now create weavings with the more realistic, three-dimensional treatment of the figures. (FIG. 22) In addition to Navajo subject matter, the Nez family also produces forest, Plains Indian, and even dinosaur pictorials.

The pattern commonly called the "tree of life," or bird pictorial, first appeared around 1900. Although its provenance is unclear, this pattern may have been derived from certain sandpainting designs. The weavings show birds perched on corn stalks, trees, or generic plants, sometimes with the vegetation growing out of a Navajo wedding basket. (FIG. 23)

A new type of pictorial was created in the Burnham, New Mexico, region in the late 1970s. It was first produced by Helen Begay who, along with her relatives in both the Barber and Begay families, created a most unusual style. It includes many different pictorial elements, such as Yé'ii, thunderbirds, and human figures mixed in with geometric designs. Burnham-style textiles usually have backgrounds using the Two Grey Hills color palette and are woven in combinations of natural wool, home-dyed, and commercially dyed colors. The geometric patterns themselves may be asymmetrical, an uncommon feature in Navajo weavings. Jackson Clark II of Toh-atin in Durango,Colorado, purchased and promoted most of the early works of Helen Begay and her family. Only time will tell whether or not this style becomes a permanent part of the Navajo weaver's repertoire. (FIG. 24)

Figure 24. Burnham weaving by Sandra Begay. 30 x 27 in. Note the three different types of Yé'ii as well as the similar but not identical side panels showing Two Grey Hills influence.

SPECIAL TECHNIQUES AND SHAPES

Several special weaving techniques make up another group of Navajo textiles. One of the best known is the raised outline weaving. The earliest known example of this type was woven in the Ganado area in 1934, but the area most associated with this technique is Coal Mine Mesa, Arizona. In 1950, Ned Hatathli helped develop it there through a project of the Navajo Arts and Crafts Guild where he was the manager. In raised outline weaving, all or most of the rug is filled with fine vertical pinstripes of various colors. Raised three-dimensional ridges outline the edges of the design elements. The ridges occur only on one side of the piece, creating a definite front and back. The effect is almost one of viewing the rug through a set of narrow bars and is more impressive with diagonal patterns. Many raised outline weavings are storm pattern rugs produced not only because of their diagonal elements but for their familiarity to Western Reservation weavers, as well.

In the 1980s, a newer variety of raised outline rug incorporated Teec Nos Pos patterns (fairly diagonal in nature) with soft, vegetal-looking colors (although most are not vegetal-dyed). (FIG. 25) This variety has been called "New Lands" by some, most notably by the trader who helped develop it, Bruce Burnham of Sanders, Arizona. He says Marie Watson Nez, working with trader Bruce McGee (then of Keam's Canyon, Arizona), created the first such weaving. Fortunately for Burnham, many Coal Mine Mesa weavers (including Wanda Begay and her family) were relocated to the New Lands area near Sanders by the mid 1980s. This was a result of the Hopi-Navajo land settlement that moved families (of both tribes) who had been living on the other tribes' territories.

Two-faced weaving is a technique requiring especially patient and talented weavers. It demands an intricate set up of the loom with a minimum of four sheds (as opposed to the normal two), each controlling different combinations of warps. (See the next chapter for a discussion of the Navajo loom.) Two-faced rugs date back to the nineteenth century. Today they are generally a diamond-twill weave surrounding panels of plain weave, bead stitch, or, occasionally, geometric designs on one side and the reverse diamond-twill weave around Yé'ii or geometric-design panels on the other. (FIG. 26)

Figure 25. Raised outline weaving by Marietta Blackrock. 51 x 35½ in. This is a very clear example of an intricate Teec Nos Pos pattern using the raised outline technique.

Figure 26. Two-faced weaving by Harriet Snyder. 44½ x 23½ in. The red background behind the Yé'ii and the geometric designs on the front panels contrasts particularly well with the grey background of the geometric patterns on the back panels.

Diamond- and diagonal-twill weavings also require multiple sheds, three or more. (See the next chapter for a full explanation of weaving techniques.) Unfortunately, while both two-faced and twill weavings are technically difficult to accomplish, the prices received for producing them have not increased proportionately compared to other weavings. As buyers look for more variety in pattern, they often ignore these seemingly repetitious but nonetheless highly intricate rugs. Hence, both the two-faced and the diamond- and diagonal-twill types are disappearing.

Tapestry weavings are considered some of the most technically demanding works ever created by Navajo weavers. A tapestry weave is currently defined as 80 wefts (the visible threads going across the face of the weaving) per linear inch, whereas the average Navajo weaving is 25 to 40 wefts per inch. The technique was developed at Two Grey Hills in the 1940s by the late Daisy Tauglechee who was capable of creating tapestries with over 120 wefts to the inch. While they are now produced in other regions, most of the finest still come from Two Grey Hills. (FIGS. 3 and 10)

Innovative Navajo weavers occasionally weave round rugs and cross-shaped styles of rug. Rose Owens is generally recognized as the round rug creator. In the late 1960s, she dreamed about Spider Woman (who the Navajo believe taught them to weave) weaving in a circle. Owen's husband brought her the metal rim of a wagon wheel to create the round shape. (FIG. 27) It is unknown when cross-shaped rugs first appeared, but they certainly existed by the mid twentieth century. (FIG. 28) Weavers of both shapes usually will not divulge their secrets, for fear of being copied.

MISCELLANEOUS PATTERNS

Sampler, or multiple-pattern rugs with designs of many different styles woven into the same rug, first appeared in the Transitional Period. For many years four-in-one rugs (four patterns on one weaving) were the most common form of sampler, although nine-in-one, fifteen-in-one, and other multiples are also seen. (FIG. 29) Another variation is the so-called rug-in-a-rug, where one

Figure 27. Round weaving by Mary H. Yazzie. 68 in. diameter.
A round rug can use any pattern. This one is primarily a Ganado regional style.

Figure 28. Cross-shaped weaving by Alice Begay, circa 1985. 48½ x 47 in.
The initial set-up of the loom creates this unique shape.

Figure 29. Four-in-one weaving by Priscilla Endischee. 42 x 28½ in.
The textile includes (clockwise from the upper left): storm pattern,
Teec Nos Pos, Ganado, and bird pictorial styles.

pattern is symmetrically centered over what appears to be another rug beneath it (often with a banded pattern). In some cases, the inner "rug" may even have tassels projecting from each corner on the front of the rug, heightening the illusion of a rug in a rug. (FIG. 30)

As in the past, Navajo weavers continue to produce revival patterns today. Especially popular are re-creations of Classic Period chief's and wearing blankets. (FIGS. 3 and 31) A newer trend developing in the 1990s has been a revival of weavings using the Germantown Transitional Period styles and colors. (FIG. 32)

Figure 30. Rug-in-a-rug weaving by Priscilla Nelwood. 38½ x 27 in.
A storm pattern rug seems to lie on top of a Wide Ruins weaving in this example.

Figure 31. Classic wearing blanket revival weaving by Gladys Shepherd. 62½ x 41½ in. This piece is based on styles prevalent during the 1860s.

Figure 32. Germantown revival weaving by Sally Scott. 72 x 52 in. Chief's blanket influences with Germantown-type colors are both evident in this textile.

UTILITARIAN WEAVINGS

We should also say a word about blankets for everyday use. In the Transitional Period, soft, loosely woven, striped blankets were produced for common uses, while the fancier wearing blankets were made to sell, to trade, or for special occasions. Saddle blankets in double (approximately 60 x 30 inches) or single size (30 x 30 inches) are often similar in weave and striping to the older utilitarian weavings. The Navajo certainly continue to weave saddle blankets for use on their own horses, but most are sold to non-Indians, often for use on the floor rather than a horse. (FIG. 33)

Gallup throws, woven and distributed primarily in the Gallup, New Mexico, area, are also loosely woven. They show simple patterning of various types and are designed primarily for floor usage. Most of them have an exposed cotton warp fringe on one end. (FIG. 34)

The tufted weave rug is a more unusual type. Alternate strands of goat hair are woven in with the weft threads to give a one-sided, shaggy rug. Tufted weave rugs are used both as saddle blankets and as sitting cushions while weaving. (FIG. 35)

We have tried to give a brief overview of the vast array of weavings that Navajo artists are producing today. Constant change permeates all styles of Navajo weaving, so categorization will continue to evolve. Hopefully, we have given the buyer some basic knowledge to identify regional, pattern, and functional styles when looking at a roomful of rugs.

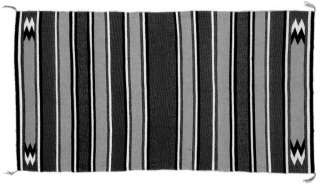

Figure 33. Double saddle blanket by Elvina Yellow. 58½ x 31 in. Typically, pattern elements are only placed in the corners or ends for visibility when used under a saddle.

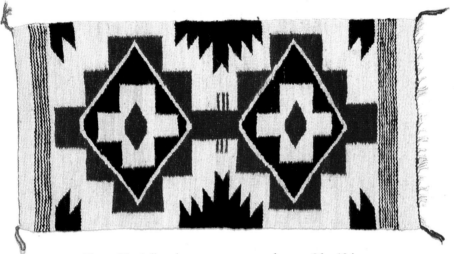

Figure 34. Gallup throw rug, weaver unknown. 36 x 18 in.
Note the cotton warp exposed at one end of the rug.

Figure 35. Tufted weave rug by Elsie Nez. 25½ x 22 in. This weaving is somewhat
unusual in that it has a pattern on the back.

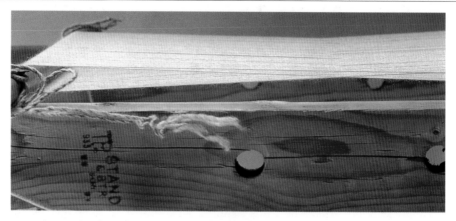

Figure 36. This side view shows the unique figure-eight structure of the warp of a Navajo weaving stretched on temporary beams.

Figure 37. The edge-cord binding which will be the finished end of the rug.

Figure 38. Lacing, end bindings, and warp structure on the permanent warp beam, with the temporary beam still in place.

THE ART OF THE NAVAJO LOOM

ONE OF THE REASONS NAVAJO weavings have been studied and admired for so long, in addition to their great beauty, is their remarkable durability. This is due primarily to their unique construction. Unlike the products of any other type of loom, Navajo weavings have four closed selvage edges. Other looms can produce only two. What this means is: no loose ends, no fringe, and no weak points at the edges of the weaving. The process of doing this is unbelievably tedious, however, and requires years to master. Hence, the difficulty of the process and the time involved in accomplishing the closed-edge phenomenon are major factors in the cost of a well-executed Navajo rug.

Working on a sturdy and usually rectangular frame (once logs or tree branches, now finished lumber or steel pipe), the weaver strings a continuous, single strand of warp in figure-eight turns around two temporary beams. (FIG. 36) The ends of these turns are then bound together with larger extra-strength, edge-cord yarns, (FIG. 37) which are then laced to permanent loom beams. (FIG. 38) The consistency of tension and spacing during these first three steps is vital to the quality of the finished product. Only with a well-done warp is there any possibility of a quality rug, since the best weaver on earth could not produce a good weaving on a bad warp. It is the spacing of the warp turns, as well as the diameter of the warp and the weft (or "weaving") yarns, which primarily determine the fineness (in terms of texture and weft rows per inch) of the rug. Warps per inch may vary from as few as four or five to as many as twenty.

Once warping is complete, the weaver places the loom in its upright position and secures one or more *heddles* and a *shed stick* in place. These are slender sticks or dowels that lift alternate sets of warps, allowing the weaver access to the spaces (known as sheds) through which to pass the weft. The warp is then stretched to the desired tension using a simple cinch rope (or small metal turnbuckles), and the actual process of weaving may begin.

We should note here that the Navajo loom is quite different from the looms used by all other weaving cultures. The lack of any automated parts (foot pedals, machine-made heddles, beater bars, shuttles, tension cranks, etc.), so common on other looms, requires of the Navajo weaver a labor-intensive procedure which is unimaginable to most other weavers. A Navajo rug is literally produced totally by hand. The "machine" that is the loom never stands between the weaver and the wool. (See back cover photograph.)

In most Navajo rugs, the basic technique employed is known as *tapestry weave*. This means "over one warp, under one warp," not a rug you hang on the wall. By this definition, all Navajo weavings (except twill, raised outline, and two-faced rugs) are tapestries. However, the term is also used by most rug dealers and collectors to designate super-fine weavings. (See chapter three.)

As the weaver works, he or she uses a batten (a smooth, flat, slightly pointed stick) to hold the sheds open for the passage of the weft. Each strand of yarn is laid in individually and beaten into place with a wooden fork or comb. (FIG. 39) In a rug of even average complexity, there may be many dozens of color changes (each requiring a different weft) on virtually every row. A typical contemporary piece (60 inches long, for example) may have anywhere from about 1,800 to 3,000 rows of weft.

Figure 39. The weaver's tools. Bottom left to top right: forks, needles, battens, Navajo hip spindle, and tow cards, shown on a Germantown revival weaving by Priscilla Warren. 36½ x 27 in.

This individual placement of the yarns creates the pattern. Each weft is woven back and forth by hand only within its own color area, interlocking with neighboring colors. (On shuttle looms, used by most non-Navajo weavers, wefts are usually carried all the way across the width of the fabric, appearing on the back of the weaving wherever they do not show on the face.) It is this process that creates the reversible effect in Navajo weaving which many find so remarkable. With few exceptions, both sides are identical.

One of the most difficult aspects of Navajo weaving involves the fact that, as the weaving nears completion, the space within which the weaver must work grows smaller and tighter. Consequently, the weaver must use a series of ever smaller tools until finally only needles fit. (FIG. 40) The rug is finished, literally, one stitch at a time. Because of this labor-intensive process, the last few inches may require many days to complete. At this point, the difficulty may tempt the weaver to put in fewer rows, lessening the tightness of the finished product. But the experienced weaver recognizes that a "good finish" is one of the qualities sought by knowledgeable buyers.

The most frequently asked question we hear is: "How long does it take to weave a rug?" There is no single answer. It takes as long as it takes. Fineness of yarn, intricacy of pattern, and the size of the rug will all affect the time required. The health, strength, and age of the weaver also play a part; and some weavers simply work faster than others. The ultimate point, of course, must be the quality of the piece, not the speed of production. Suffice it to say that a Navajo weaver thinks not in terms of the hours, but of the months that the rug will be on the loom.

Figure 40. Curved needle used to carry the final wefts between the warps.

A point to consider regarding the time involved in a particular weaving is the source of the yarn. A weaver who prepares yarn "from scratch" has invested an enormous amount of time before the weaving of the rug has even begun. Shearing, washing, carding, spinning, and dying wool (not to mention gathering and preparing dyestuffs) is slow and tedious work. Homespun Navajo yarn is prepared on a simple hip spindle. (FIG. 39) The Navajo have never accepted the European spinning wheel, primarily because it is not as portable as the spindle. It is difficult to herd a flock of sheep while carrying a spinning wheel. Unfortunately, the time required for home production of yarn is rarely adequately reflected in the price received for the rug.

STANDARDS OF QUALITY

Purchasing a Navajo rug can be a confusing and intimidating experience. Unless you are an expert, you must be able to rely on dealers. Find one or two dealers in quality weavings who have done their homework and know good from bad. They should be able to demonstrate and explain the differences of styles, yarns, weavers, and the like. Check out their reputation, experience, quality of selection, etc. A knowledgable dealer can tell you, for example, why two rugs of the same size, that may appear similar in design, have vastly different prices. If they cannot, go elsewhere! Ultimately, it is up to the prospective buyer to read, look, and ask questions. In this way, you can then be confident in your own knowledge and of the reliability of your dealer.

In judging the technical quality of any contemporary Navajo weaving, we advise that these standards be applied:

1. *Does the rug have straight edges and square corners?* It is surprising how often this is not the case. While total straightness and squareness is the ideal, completely straight sides are a rarity. To those accustomed to machine-made products, this may seem strange. In handweaving, however, one of the most difficult aspects to master is the control of a "clean" (straight and consistent) edge. Keep in mind also that the longer the rug, the harder it is to maintain a perfect edge and the more forgiving one must be. (However, parallelogram or trapezoid-shaped rugs should be strictly avoided.) Check by folding the weaving to see that both ends are the same width.

2. *Are the pattern lines within the rug straight and consistent?* Keeping long lines (both horizontal and vertical) straight and even while weaving can be quite difficult. With horizontal lines, the slightest variance in the spacing of the warp and/or texture or diameter of the weft can cause a line to waver. Long vertical lines, even more than horizontals, are exceedingly tricky for the weaver to deal with. They have a tendency to become uneven in width and loose in texture. Control over both indicates great skill by the weaver.

3. *Is the pattern centered on the rug?* This may sound simplistic, yet placing the center of the pattern in the exact center of the rug is much more difficult than usually imagined. Horizontal placement can be problematic (if warps are not spaced consistently), but is relatively simple compared to the nightmare of vertical centering. The weaving line in progress is always higher than it will be later because the last several rows, although already beaten down with the fork, remain somewhat loose until compacted by more weaving above them. Since the warp is wool, it continues to stretch throughout the process, constantly changing the length of the rug. Humidity also makes warps stretch. The weaver must consider all of these factors in determining the placement of the center of the pattern. Expertise comes only through years of experience.

Figure 41. Master weaver Barbara Teller Ornelas at her loom working on a Two Grey Hills tapestry, with a chief's blanket also in progress on another loom.

4. *Will the rug lie (or hang) flat?* As a general rule, avoid rugs with seriously curled corners, puckered edges, or "ripples" in the body of the weaving. Corner and side problems of this nature may or may not be correctable by an experienced restoration weaver. Ripples and puckers in the interior portion of the rug are usually impossible to fix. Do not be overly concerned about fold marks. Space limitations in most retail galleries require the folding of most rugs. Creases at the fold points will usually soon disappear. For ways to get rid of creases faster, ask your dealer. At this point, we must stress that a weaving should always be examined flat on the floor or hanging on the wall. Never purchase a piece that is shown only folded or draped. In addition, always view the piece as you intend to use it (a floor rug on the floor, a wall hanging on the wall). Minor flaws that may not be noticeable on the floor may be glaringly apparent on the wall.

5. *Is the warp covered?* In the ideal Navajo rug, the warp will be completely hidden. There are forgiveable exceptions. Tiny bits of warp showing at the ends of the rug (where the body of the weaving meets the end binding cords) are almost inevitable. Likewise, some visible warp "dots" along the line of a horizontal movement of color, though not desirable, are forgiveable. Much exposed warp in solid color areas is the result of poor workmanship and should be avoided.

6. *Are there visibly noticeable "lazy lines?"* "Lazy lines" (inaccurately named by those who did not understand their function) are diagonal joints in the weaving. They allow the weaver to work on a section of the rug for a period of time without having to move back and forth the full width of the rug on every row. A skilled weaver will insure that these joints are either totally invisible or at least barely noticeable in the finished product. Lazy lines have long been an accepted part of Navajo weaving technique. However, they should never be visibly distracting in a contemporary weaving.

7. *Are the colors consistent?* This is usually not a problem with contemporary weavings. Noticeable color changes can occur if the weaver neglects to purchase or produce enough of the same dye lot of a given color to complete the pattern in the rug. Visible color changes may become quite distracting over time. (In older weavings, color changes are a common occurance.)

In examining a piece for all of the above factors, the buyer must also consider the price. While the same standards are used to judge all weavings, they obviously must be applied more strictly to more expensive pieces. Flaws which may be somewhat forgiveable in a $500 textile are not in a $5,000 one. Keep in mind also that the older the piece, the more lenient the application of the standards. The level of technical expertise demanded in Navajo weavings has constantly risen over the past hundred years.

We should make a point here about budget. In our opinion, the buyer should usually seek out the highest affordable level of quality. It is better to have a very fine, smaller weaving than a larger but poorly woven one.

While all of the standards of quality are important, never overlook the emotional appeal of the piece. The artistic factor is paramount. If you love the rug enough, it was meant to be yours. However, you must love it in spite of (and knowing) its technical imperfections. Flaws discovered after the rug is home can destroy your initial fondness for the weaving.

Try to avoid the pitfalls of "mystique." There are a number of persistent misconceptions (perpetuated, at least in part, by the sales pitches of some clerks and dealers) regarding Navajo weavings. A classic example is symbolism. With the exception of Yé'ii, Yé'ii Bichei, and sandpainting rugs, there is very little symbolic meaning behind the designs found in Navajo weavings. For the most part, they are simply pretty patterns. While individual design elements may have acquired names over the years, these usually came about after the fact, due to a general resemblance to some object familiar to the viewer. Such a resemblance is usually coincidental, rather than intentional on the part of the weaver.

One very notable exception to the rule of no symbolism is the so-called swastika found in some rugs woven prior to World War II. To the Navajo, it is the "whirling logs," a geometric stylization of a design derived from certain sandpaintings integral to their religious healing ceremonies.

Another myth is the intentional flaw. This simply does not exist in Navajo weaving. It may be true that some Oriental rug-weaving cultures believe that "only God can make something perfect," and therefore their weavers introduce an intentional flaw into the pattern of each rug. This is certainly not true among Navajo weavers. Almost any Navajo weaving, if examined closely enough, will reveal at least one flaw, but this is not due to any religious taboo.

It is because weavers are human and humans make mistakes.

The buyer must not confuse flaws, intentional or otherwise, with the phenomenon known as the spirit line (also called the spirit trail or weaver's pathway). This is a tiny line of weft yarn which allows the "escape" of the primary background color directly through all pattern and border colors to the edge of the rug. The line is usually woven in at the point of the background color nearest to the right-hand edge of the rug as the weaver approaches the end of the weaving. (FIG. 42) Weavers will tell you that this exit is to the east. One theory states that in the days when much weaving was done outside (there is very little light in a traditional Navajo home, or *hogan*), a weaver would naturally orient the loom so that it faced south. The sun would then be at the artist's back, not in the eyes. This would mean that "to the right" was "to the east." Openings, as perceived in Navajo culture (in sandpaintings and hogans, for example), are always to the east.

We should note here that the spirit line is a phenomenon essentially brought about by non-Indian traders. As explained previously, Navajo weavings did not originally include borders but were always open-sided designs. (FIGS. 1 and 2) It was the early traders who, probably unaware of the taboo against things being closed in, asked the weavers for borders. They believed (accurately, as it turned out) that this would increase saleability. The weavers, whose very livelihood depended on these traders, naturally included the desired borders, but avoided possible misfortune by incorporating the spirit line. Interestingly, the spirit line seems to be much more prevalent on the eastern side of the reservation than in the central or western regions. For example, Two Grey Hills weavings almost always incorporate a spirit line, whereas Ganado (central) and storm pattern rugs (western) often do not. Today some

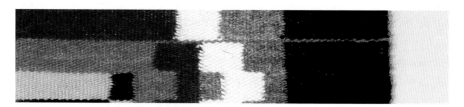

Figure 42. Close-up of a spirit line in a Two Grey Hills weaving by Dorothy Lowe.
Note the extension of the spirit line from the brown background through the
pattern and border colors to the rug's edge.

weavers include it because they believe in the taboo. Others say, "because Mom taught me to." As one weaver states, including spirit lines "is an interesting thing to talk about" when selling the rug.

CARING FOR YOUR WEAVINGS

Once you have found and adopted the rug that was meant to be yours, you must assume the responsibilities of being its keeper. Do not panic. The "care and feeding" of a Navajo rug is not difficult. There are, however, a few dos and don'ts which you must remember.

Don't ever wash a Navajo weaving! No matter what you may have heard or read about pioneers scrubbing their rugs in the snow, do not ever consider getting water on your rug. (Yes, they did scrub them, and yes, they did ruin them.) Wool is an organic material and all of the various types of cords that make up a Navajo rug (warps, wefts, selvages) will react differently to liquids. Some stretch, some contract. Water may cause puckers and ripples, or worse. Such damage to the basic foundation of the rug is often irreparable.

Don't snap or beat a Navajo rug. This can damage the natural fibers, also. At most, shake the rug gently, holding it only by the sides and never the ends.

Do vacuum the rug. Again, as wool is organic, it must be kept free of insect larvae and other potentially damaging dirt and debris. If the rug is on the wall, it should be taken down and gently vacuumed on both sides at least every six months. If on the floor, it will usually require more frequent cleaning. Use upholstery attachments, never a beater brush. Eventually, all floor rugs and some wall hangings may need professional cleaning. Check with your dealer for a reliable cleaner near you. If this is not possible, seek out the closest reputable cleaner of fine Oriental carpets and rugs (preferably one who has experience with Navajo textiles).

Do consider texture and traffic. Whenever a rug is used on the floor, the conditions and traffic of that area must be compatible with the tightness and thickness of the weaving. A rug that may be suitable in a guest bedroom, for example, may not wear well in an entryway.

Do rotate rugs periodically. Floor rugs should be turned in a different direction every time you vacuum. Wall hangings should be rotated (top to bottom, front to back) at six-month intervals when you take the rug down for vacuuming. We also recommend that rugs be given a *light* "misting" with a moth-proofing spray at this time. (Remember that moths, silverfish, and especially crickets are your enemies.) Hold the spray *at least 2 feet away* from the weaving to avoid getting too much chemical residue on the piece.

Do use pads under floor rugs. Even on smooth floors, a minimum-thickness foam or felt (not plastic mesh), non-skid mat should be used to prevent sliding. On floors with any irregularities (tile, etc.), put down thicker pads.

Don't position floor rugs under heavy, abrasive, or sharp-edged pieces of furniture. If such placement is absolutely necessary, use furniture-leg cups and rotate the rug much more frequently.

Do use Velcro if the weaving is to be used as a wall hanging. In years past, rug collectors were forced to do terrible things to their rugs in order to hang them. Now, thanks to the inventor of Velcro (who, it is said, was inspired by a thistle caught on his trousers), hanging a rug is neither difficult nor damaging to the fabric. Rug Velcro is different from clothing Velcro. Unlike the two-sided fasteners used on clothing and shoes, where one side has "hooks" and one has "loops," rug Velcro requires only the hooks. (The wool of the rug acts as the loops.) Rug Velcro is usually wider, for a better hold on larger rugs. It has an adhesive backing which adheres directly to the wall. The Velcro may also be stapled, nailed, or tacked to the wall (with its backing) to avoid lifting paint with the adhesive. (Note: Sometimes old rugs are polished so smooth from use that they will not grip the Velcro. In such cases, see your dealer for possible alternatives.)

Don't hang a weaving with nails, brads, staples, or "tack-strip" piercing the rug. Any such intrusion in the fabric of the rug is potentially very damaging. Metal points may puncture or tear the yarn, or may rust, causing permanent discoloration. No matter how closely spaced, such points of suspension will eventually cause areas of sag in between. This stretching, much like the damage from washing, is irreparable. An alternative means of hanging rugs involves two wooden presser bars (much like old-fashioned men's pants hangers). The problem with these is that they, too, may eventually leave permanent impressions on the rug.

Don't frame Navajo rugs under glass, plexiglass, or any other material which will prevent the natural "breathing" of the wool. Weavings which are sealed in may develop problems from mold, mildew, insects, etc. Additionally, don't ever allow a framer to glue a Navajo weaving to any sort of backing or matting. This prevents all maintenance and will destroy any value which the piece may once have had. There are acceptable methods of framing rugs, which will vary depending on the particulars of the piece. Check with your dealer regarding those techniques best suited to your needs.

Don't store rugs for any length of time unless it is absolutely necessary. If so, never store them folded, but always rolled. Rugs should be rolled from end to end, never from side to side and, if possible, should be rolled around something, such as a cardboard tube, to prevent excessive curling on the inside end. The rolled weaving should then be wrapped in acid-free tissue paper, white or brown wrapping paper, or a clean, plain white bed sheet. Never store a rug wrapped in plastic, as plastic can allow moisture to condense on the inside.

Do protect stored rugs against moths and other insects. Cedar-lined chests or closets are ideal. Otherwise, use moth spray (see above), flakes or balls, remembering to replenish these at six-month intervals. (Keep in mind that moth flakes and balls should never actually touch the rug.)

If problems occur with your rug, do not despair. Most can be remedied. Removal of stains and soiling is usually possible through proper cleaning. Discoloration due to the running of certain dyes in some old rugs (almost never a problem in contemporary weavings) can often be removed by a process called de-bleeding. Structural damage (some curling and rippling, holes, puppy-chewed corners, worn edges, etc.) can be remedied by a knowledgeable restoration weaver. Never allow anyone to repair your Navajo rug using sewing techniques such as darning. Such work must be undertaken only by those who have the necessary skills to fully restore Navajo weavings.Check with your dealer for assistance in locating a reputable restoration weaver.

Don't let these few requirements discourage you. The time and effort involved in properly caring for a fine rug is minimal. The pleasure such a piece will bring is vast. Above all, remember: Navajo weaving today is an art form and should be viewed, used, and appreciated as such.

Detail of the raised outline weaving in Figure 25.

INNOVATION AND THE FUTURE

Over the years, the process of weaving a Navajo textile and the loom on which it is created have changed very little. The look and function, however, have undergone dramatic transformations. These changes have paved the way for an exciting future for the art of Navajo weaving.

As we have pointed out, Navajo women originally began weaving to make clothing and blankets to wear. Over time, these items were used as trade goods and, still later, as products to sell. Today, economic considerations have become the prime motivating factor in the continuation of Navajo weaving. This is not to deny that some artists, like Pearl Ben of Sweetwater, Arizona, weave in part because it is a hobby. Like others, she also weaves to continue the age-old tradition of weaving as part of the Navajo woman's role. Artists like Barbara Teller Ornelas, originally from Two Grey Hills, New Mexico, have an almost physical need to weave. She says, "Weaving is in my soul....I do not feel right unless a rug is on the loom." Artistic expression is often another goal. For some weavers, the creative process itself is a reward totally apart from the financial one. Still, most Navajo weavers would not continue if they could not earn money in the process.

Creating a rug is a long and arduous task; hence, any time- or labor-saving innovations are of the utmost importance. The single most important change in this area has been the widespread distribution of commercially spun and dyed wool yarn. Two companies most responsible for this development were Brown's Sheep Company of Mitchell, Nebraska, and John B. Wilde & Brother of Philadelphia, Pennsylvania. These companies now provide the vast majority of yarn used in Navajo textiles. Brown's started selling yarn in the Shiprock area around 1980. At first they offered only four colors, but the palette rapidly expanded and now includes many vegetal-looking shades. Today, according to Harlan Brown, about one-third of their yarn goes to Navajo weavers, distributed through several traders on the reservation.

The entrance of the Wilde company into the Navajo market came from a collaboration with trader Bruce Burnham of Sanders, Arizona. In the early 1980s, Burnham worked with Wilde's (in business since 1880) to produce what he calls "carpet yarn" that the weavers could use. They, too, started with about four colors but now make many hues. Burnham markets the yarn under the name "Wilde & Wooly." Some of it is home-dyed by Navajo women using vegetal dyes, as well as mixtures from other sources in a multitude of shades. We have heard of weavers using Kool Aid, grape juice, crepe paper, and lady's rouge, among others, in their dyes. Wilde & Wooly yarn is available in four weights from fine tapestry to saddle-blanket thickness. Wilde's Russ Fawley acknowledges that the Navajo segment of their sales is relatively small but important.

Burnham and Wilde are also currently marketing three-ply Germantown yarns in bright, old-style colors that duplicate the look of Transitional Period yarns, specifically for weavers wishing to create Germantown revival rugs. Unfortunately, unscrupulous individuals may try to age contemporary weavings using this yarn, in the hope of extracting a high price for a fake "antique."

People often seem surprised to learn the extent to which most Navajo weavers use commercially prepared yarn in their rugs. Most traders estimate that about 95% of all contemporary Navajo weavings contain commercial yarns. It is difficult for many people to distinguish it from handspun yarn, but a knowledgeable and reputable salesperson should be able to show the buyer the difference. A buyer should assume that a contemporary rug does not contain handspun yarn unless it is specifically proven otherwise. Many dealers do not divulge this fact to their customers because of the romance of handspun and dyed yarns and fear of negative reactions to commercial ones. People forget that the Germantown yarns used well over a hundred years ago were also completely commercially manufactured, yet the rugs containing them are now very valuable.

Most important is the fact that there would be few Navajo rugs around today if weavers were not using commercial yarns. Making a living from weaving would be virtually impossible without them. The process of carding, spinning, and dying wool takes a tremendous amount of time and significantly reduces the ratio of money received to effort spent. The elimination of wool preparation before weaving has also allowed artists the flexibility to focus on more intricate designs and to create some of the most consistently textured and evenly finished rugs ever made. Nevertheless, handspun yarn has a strong traditional appeal, and it is unfortunate that the few weavers who still prepare their own wool are not compensated adequately for their extra labor.

Unlike potters or Hopi kachina doll carvers, Navajo weavers rarely sign their pieces. Most buyers cannot tell one artist's textiles from another's. Thus, in the last few years some traders have attempted to induce artists to weave in signatures (whether letters or symbols), usually in one corner of the piece. So far this signing is limited to a very small number of weavers. Most Navajo have resisted, since anonymity (which safeguards the power associated with one's name) and non-competitiveness are both deep-seated traditions. Some traders regularly insist on signatures when they purchase a rug. It may one day become common practice, given the Anglo preference for signed artwork of all kinds. (FIGS. 43 and 44)

For centuries, women produced almost all Navajo weavings. At least one unidentified male weaver was working in the nineteenth century. Hosteen Klah (mentioned earlier) wove in the early twentieth century. Until recently, though, it was still rare to find a Navajo man at the loom. This was partly due to the fact that the Navajo considered weaving part of a woman's traditional

Figure 43. Close-up of a letter signature in a Yé'ii weaving by Ruby White.

Figure 44. Close-up of a feather as a symbol signature in a Burntwater weaving by LaRose Bia.

Figure 45. Teec Nos Pos weaving by Jason Harvey. 52 x 34 in.
The black background is unusual in this region.
In addition to the intricate pattern, Harvey has used a
superfine weave of about 56 wefts per inch.

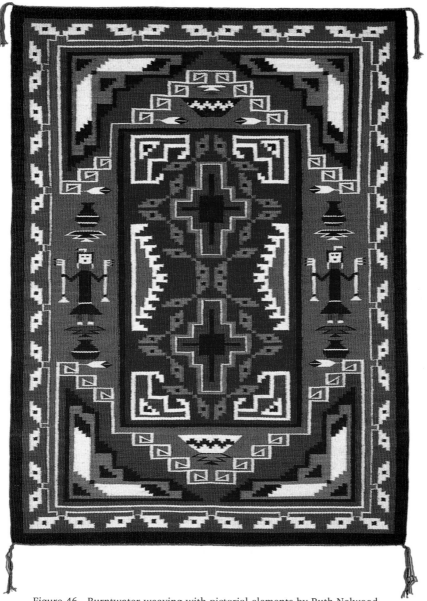

Figure 46. Burntwater weaving with pictorial elements by Ruth Nelwood.
46½ x 35½ in. Note the Yé'ii, basket, and pottery figures along the sides,
as well as the rug-in-a-rug feeling of the piece.

knowledge and hence not a "manly" thing to do. Many men who wove in the past sold their rugs under their wives' names to avoid this stigma. Some still do so today, but more male artists are taking up weaving to bring in income for their families. In some cases, daughters have not carried on the tradition of their mothers, but sons have. Nowadays, most regions have at least one or two male weavers. One such weaver is Albert Jackson, now of Red Valley, Arizona. Being a male, he was not expected to weave but at about age six became interested in the process. He says, "One day while my family was away, I snuck some yarn to try to weave." When his grandmother and mother discovered his desire to learn, they agreed to teach him. He says that today female weavers respect his talents.

As with most Native American crafts, art has crossed gender lines. Kachina doll carving is no longer an all-male domain, and pottery is no longer an all-female one. More men are finding creative expression through weaving than ever before, and now most are willing to take credit for it. (FIG. 45)

Another important innovation in Navajo weaving at the end of the twentieth century is the movement away from strict regional stereotypes to a combination of elements from styles of many areas. Two Grey Hills type textiles with Teec Nos Pos type borders, storm pattern weavings with sampler designs, and Burntwater style rugs with pictorial elements (FIG. 46)—all these are some of the many varieties currently emerging. The advent of better highways and transportation have affected mobility and expanded the number of designs that weavers might see. For a prolonged time, weavers were exposed only to weavings of their own regional style. Now they can gather ideas from across the reservation. As with most artists, the desire to try something new is a strong one. Of course, today's innovations will become tomorrow's traditions.

Other stylistic changes are developing with some frequency and rapidity. In about 1990, Sarah Paul Begay (working from a concept of trader Bruce McGee's, now of Holbrook, Arizona) created a textile where the background rug had what appeared to be multiple, small rugs laid randomly on top of it. The designs of the small rugs all overlapped one another so only portions of each were visible. Other weavers are now creating similar variations of this sampler rug. (FIG. 47)

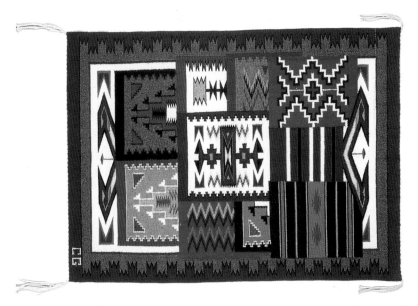

Figure 47. Sampler weaving by Cecilia George. 47 x 34 in.
The background rug is a Teec Nos Pos pattern.

Figure 48. Raised outline "Blue Canyon" weaving by Lena Curtiss. 64 x 35 in. This textile
includes the styles of at least three different areas.

In chapter 3 we mentioned the asymmetrical patterns in the Burnham area pictorial weavings. A different asymmetrical style was first woven by the late Larry Yazzie (YAH-zee), originally from the Blue Canyon area of the Western Reservation. Yazzie came from a family with both male and female weavers. His style consisted of weaving different sections of the rug in different designs (storm patterns, Teec Nos Pos, Burntwater, etc.). He used the raised outline technique, but these variations have been called Blue Canyon rugs by their makers. Yazzie's sister, Lena Curtiss, continues this style of weaving today. Whether other weavers will break the strong Navajo tradition of symmetrical geometric rugs remains to be seen. (FIG. 48)

New styles of rugs are also emerging in southeastern Utah. One is the "mosaic" rug in which the central design element appears to lie on a fractured background. This idea was a collaboration between trader Steve Simpson, designer Susie Campbell Bell, and weaver Anita Hatathle in 1995. Other artists in the area are now making these as well. (FIG. 49) The other new creation

Figure 49. Mosaic weaving by Evelyn White. 48½ x 48½ in. White's outstanding piece won a blue ribbon at the 1996 Gallup Inter-Tribal Indian Ceremonial.

from this area is the "mythology" rug, which shows scenes from Navajo myths and legends. The original concept came from trader Barry Simpson of Blue Mountain Trading Post in Blanding. They are being interpreted from the myths by Navajo graphic artist Damian Jim on a computer, a novel use of today's technology. Several talented weavers are currently producing them. The taboos that apply to weavers of sandpainting rugs are not applicable in these rugs because the scenes do not come directly from sandpaintings. (FIG. 50)

From the Western Reservation, two new weaving types have appeared. Dinnebito (dih-NEH-bih-TOE) black rugs were first woven around 1990. They use either traditional central diamond designs as seen at Ganado and Two Grey Hills or storm patterns, but with a black background. Rose Dan Begay first created them from an idea of traders Elijah and Jim Blair, now of Page, Arizona. (FIG. 51)

The unusual Spider Woman rugs are being woven primarily near Cedar Ridge and Bitter Springs, Arizona. Rena Mountain is credited with creating them in the late 1980s. The weavings have a square or rectangular hole in the center to represent the place of emergence that Spider Woman passed through to this world. Interestingly, some nineteenth-century rugs had small central openings called Spider Woman holes. (FIG. 52)

With these many innovations, a greater appreciation and awareness of the artists as well as of the art have developed. Before the 1960s, most rugs were not even tagged with the weaver's name. Rugs were considered more of an anonymous piece of Native American decoration than a work of art by a specific Navajo individual. As better artists gained recognition for their workmanship and style, collectors began asking for their weavings by name. For example, many people now do not just ask for a tapestry weaving. They ask for a Barbara Ornelas or a Julia Jumbo tapestry weaving. Of course, any collector should remember the most important thing to look for is a quality piece, no matter who the weaver is.

So what is the future of Navajo weaving? Certainly we can expect to see more variety and inventiveness, even finer workmanship and more detailed combinations of patterns. With this increase in difficulty, higher prices for superior quality work will be the inevitable result.

The biggest problem may be the decline in the number of weavers and

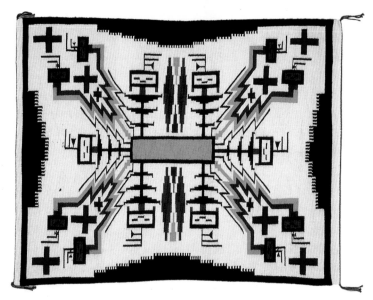

Figure 50. Mythology weaving by Christine Yazzie. 61 x 48 in.
This example depicts the Corn Spirits.

Figure 51. "Dinnebito black" weaving by Rose Dan Begay. 51 x 33½ in.

Figure 52. Spider Woman rug by Tomacita Sloan. 36 x 28 in. Note the rectangular opening (the emergence hole) in the center of the storm pattern.

weavings. Almost all traders note that fewer rugs are being made by fewer weavers every year. As we have said, rug production is heavily market-driven. Even with rug prices as seemingly high as they are today, weavers still have difficulty making a living. Like the general populace, the Navajo hold a wide variety of jobs. Unfortunately, most can even make more working at a fast-food restaurant than weaving.

One discouraging factor is that many shops choose to sell so-called Indian-design rugs from Mexico, the Orient, and other parts of the world rather than Navajo weavings. Other weaving cultures have their own unique patterns—reproducing Navajo ones strictly to make cheaper copies is ethically question-able. Potential buyers may not understand the difficulty and slowness of Navajo weaving compared to the ease and speed of techniques employed by other weavers. The qualitative differences between these weavings may also not be obvious to the uninitiated. Thus, inexpensive imitations compete directly with superior and more costly Navajo textiles. An unfortunate aspect of these knock-offs is that the seller may either intentionally misrepresent them or may encourage the customer to believe they are authentically Navajo by the use of terms like "Navajo design" or "Navajo style." The buyer should remember that the Navajo must live in our economy just as the rest of us do and cannot survive on the meager wages that workers in other countries do. It is also true that quality workmanship is available in virtually every price range of Navajo rugs, including even the least expensive pieces. However, a low price never excuses a poor-quality weaving.

Another issue is the perception that Navajo textiles are a craft rather than an art form. As Jed Foutz of Shiprock Trading Company so convincingly puts it, "How can people spend so much on Anglo paintings and then complain about the prices of Navajo weavings, which take so much longer to produce?" Because of this, Foutz is concerned that younger weavers may not continue, and that the art could lose much of its current innovation.

Trader Bruce McGee notes that for a few of the best weavers, the issue of money is less critical. For the weavers whose work is in greatest demand, traders may vie for these top-quality pieces in bidding wars. McGee recognizes that this is not true, of course, for the vast majority. Joe Tanner, a trader from Gallup, New Mexico, feels it is the trader's role to help the Navajo "come to the rug market with the best work they can do, so they will be able to meet their families' needs."

Bill Malone, who runs the Hubbell Trading Post at Ganado, thinks inexpensive rugs may virtually disappear as younger weavers will not make "cheap rugs." He says weaving is headed more towards the upper end of the price spectrum, with only the best of the best getting top dollar for their work. Robert Ingeholm of Blair's Dinnebito Trading Post in Page, Arizona, also agrees that the prices for better weavings will go up, while average-quality rugs will stay about the same. He expects to see rug production falling off more than 25% in years to come, especially among younger weavers.

Weavers, too, express concerns about where weaving is headed. Most of those we know are over forty years of age. Many seem to know a number of capable weavers, especially younger ones, who are not making or will not make rugs. Some young Navajo feel that weaving is old people's work.

In spite of the challenges, weaver Pearl Ben believes that the art of weaving will not die among the Navajo. She knows several Navajo in their twenties taking up weaving today. Albert Jackson points out that, like himself, more men are weaving than ever. Most weavers express hope that the art will be passed on to future generations, but there seems to be a sense of trepidation as well. As current weavers continue to age and younger ones do not replace them, the future of Navajo weaving may appear somewhat precarious.

We, too, feel that weaving will most likely continue. The look will change, perhaps dramatically, as it has many times in the past. The number of pieces produced may decline, but the quality may be even better. We believe this tradition of beauty and harmony will endure. An expression of this faith may best be voiced by Barbara Teller Ornelas. "I hope older weavers will be strong enough to teach younger weavers, since weaving is such an important part of being Navajo."

BIBLIOGRAPHY

Belikove, Ruth K.
1994   *The Rugs of Teec Nos Pos: Jewels of the Navajo Loom.*
        Albuquerque, NM: Adobe Gallery.

Brugge, David M.
1983   "Navajo Prehistory and History to 1850" in *Handbook of the
        North American Indians,* Vol. 10 (Alfonso Ortiz, ed.).
        Washington, DC: Smithsonian Institution.

Hedlund, Anne Lane
1992   *Reflections of the Weaver's World: The Gloria F. Ross Collection of
        Contemporary Navajo Weaving.* Denver, CO: Denver Art Museum.
1994   *"Contemporary Navajo Weaving: Thoughts That Count"*
        (*Plateau,* Vol. 65, No. 1). Flagstaff, AZ: Museum of Northern
        Arizona.

James, H. L.
1988   *Rugs and Posts: The Story of Navajo Weaving and Indian Trading.*
        Westchester, PA: Schiffer Publishing, Ltd.

Kaufman, Alice and Christopher Selser
1985   *The Navajo Weaving Tradition, 1650 to the Present.* New York: E.
        P. Dutton, Inc.

Kent, Kate Peck
1981   "From Blanket to Rug: The Evolution of Navajo Weaving after
        1880" in *Tension and Harmony: The Navajo Rug* (*Plateau,* Vol.
        52, No. 4). Flagstaff, AZ: Museum of Northern Arizona.
1985   *Navajo Weaving: Three Centuries of Change.* Santa Fe, NM:
        School of American Research Press.

Maxwell, Gilbert S.
1984   *Navajo Rugs: Past, Present and Future.* (Revision by Bill and
        Sande Bobb.) Santa Fe, NM: Heritage Art.

McGreevy, Susan Brown

1994   *The Image Weavers: Contemporary Navajo Pictorial Textiles.*
Santa Fe, NM: Wheelwright Museum of the American Indian.

Mera, H. P. and Joe Ben Wheat

1978   *The Alfred I. Barton Collection of Southwestern Textiles.* Coral
Gables, FL: Lowe Art Museum, University of Miami.

Moore, J. B.

1986   *The Navajo.* Albuquerque, NM: Avanyu Publishing, Inc.

Roessel, Jr., Robert A.

1983   "Navajo History, 1850-1923" in *Handbook of North American
Indians*, Vol. 10 (Alfonso Ortiz, ed.). Washington, DC:
Smithsonian Institution.

Wheat, Joe Ben

1981   "Early Navajo Weaving" in *Tension and Harmony: The Navajo
Rug* (*Plateau*, Vol. 52, No. 4). Flagstaff, AZ: Museum of Northern
Arizona.

1984   *The Gift of Spiderwoman: Southwestern Textiles and the Navajo
Tradition.* Philadelphia: The University Museum, University of
Pennsylvania.

INDEX